SALT SHAKER GIRLS

Elizabeth McMunn-Tetangco

Salt Shaker Girls

First Printing

ISBN 978-1-970860-96-2

Cover Art Credit: Elizabeth McMunn-Tetangco

*to my family
and my Fontainebleau text thread*

SALT SHAKER GIRLS

a kiss is still a kiss backyard fruit trees

the wilderness
just on its edge
work parking lot

my thoughts wilt
in the heat
lake afternoon

wine bottles
hung on strings
her face in mine

las vegas airport
all the planes
lined up to leave

soft snow
down to one blanket
on the bed

the uber driver
plays sinatra
early flight

first day of spring
the dogs unearth
a buried toy

the cherry in his cocktail
turning brown
funeral lunch

on the floor
a glitter heart
hotel bar

the bent joints
of fried chicken legs
her anger

weak stars
the number
on the lost dog's tag

submerged
in hot tub water
my rough edges

all the different kinds
of buttons
women's bodies

long marriage
the whole sky
tucked round itself

laying white flowers
on her casket
sideways rain

sword swallower
this shape I hide
inside

the cashier thinks
that we're a couple
the deer's head in sunglasses

his heart
changing its shape
afternoon latte

hospice care
the courtyard room
already taken

overwintering
he turns the furnace back
to on

fingernail moon
whatever we were
still a secret

insurance papers
my old password still
his name

sciatica
the TV baseball player's
pant stripe

micromoon my shoes still full of sand

how hot it feels
inside
lion dance

single hole punch
at the end
of orange season

quiche cut
like a half moon
easter sunday

leaf shadows
in his office
after hours

freeway
a pink cow nose
sticks out from a livestock truck

whether each raindrop
has a soul
summer moths

halfway
through summer
denim dress

the taste
of canned anchovies
middle age

the hard seeds
of her sadness
loquat fruit

the lit-up pieces
of the rocket
icarus

the first hot night
our swimsuits left
outside

how much
can fit beneath them
distant mountains

cicada season
the night filling
with their secrets

spooked horse
the parade route between
his teeth

she pulls her earbuds out summer thunder

in someone's landscaping
one small gray fox
property line

summer concert
the moon's path
above the lights

tips
of the cypress trees
outlining clouds

half an **SSRI** last quarter moon

snow patches
the holes
in his story

fish market
what a life sells for
these days

the moon still
keeps its distance
partner dance

late afternoon
shadows of leaves
on the umbrella

mountain lion sighting
everyone saw
something different

free refills
the bar singer's
politics

if it's my neighbor
or a monster
halloween

our kids now grown
through trees
the milky way

lily pad meanings
the pre-op room
curtains

another
surgery the
hailstoned street

what we leave
between us
pizza crusts

red leaves
on his old street
I look for patterns

in three languages the do not enter sign

her silence
during dinner
thunderheads

all this unexpected rain special election

double lock
the loneliness
of hotel rooms

ghost town never who I hoped to see

the sound of the icemaker summer night

she asks
if it's about him
desert rabbits

a surprise to both of us the cormorant

my heart losing
its shape
seasonal latte

processing emotions
the moon in
and out of clouds

what she'll leave behind moving boxes

in a past life
white marks
on the bird's wings

letting things go the pile of leaves

half-shells
in an old drawer
our wedding favors

early dark
she pulls the heat pad
from the closet

murmuration
what it's like
in someone's marriage

line drawing
of mountains
three days' rain

high tide line the new wrinkles round her ne

here they used to collect dust salt shaker girls

ABOUT THE AUTHOR

Elizabeth McMunn-Tetangco lives in Merced, CA with her husband, son, dogs, and cats. She co-edits *First Frost* and *One Sentence Poems*.

9 781970 860962